Once I Was Very Very Scared

by Chandra Ghosh Ippen

illustrations by Erich Ippen jr.

Piplo productions

San Francisco, CA

Piploproductions.com

First edition published in 2017
ISBN: 978-0-9984126-1-0 (hardcover edition)
ISBN: 978-0-9984126-0-3 (paperback edition)

Summary: "Once I was very very scared", declares squirrel. The other animals chime in to share that they were also once scared. Through the story we learn what scared the little animals, ways they each respond when scared, and things that help them feel safe and calm. This book was designed to help young children who have experienced stressful or traumatic events.

The development of the story was funded in part by the Substance Abuse and Mental Heath Services Administration (SAMHSA), US Department of Health and Human Service (HHS). The views, policies, and opinions expressed are those of the authors and do not necessarily reflect those of SAMHSA or HHS.

Special thanks to colleagues at the Child Trauma Research Program and the National Child Traumatic Stress Network who provided feedback and support.

For grown-ups around the world who help
children feel protected and cherished,
for all the children they love,
and for Raiden, our son, who is very very loved.

Once, I was very very scared.

Me too.

Not me.
I'm never
scared.

I don't like to talk about it.

I wonder
what scared you.

The wind.
It was so loud.
It hurt my house.
My toys were broken.
The nuts went everywhere.
The whole place was shaking.

Someone I love left.
I don't like it
when people leave.
They leave a lot.

People were fighting.
I hid, but they
kept fighting.
They went on
and on.

People started yelling.
No one wanted me around.
I got scared, and I
sprayed. They yelled more,
and I sprayed more.

I don't remember
what happened,
but it was bad.
I worry bad things
might happen again.

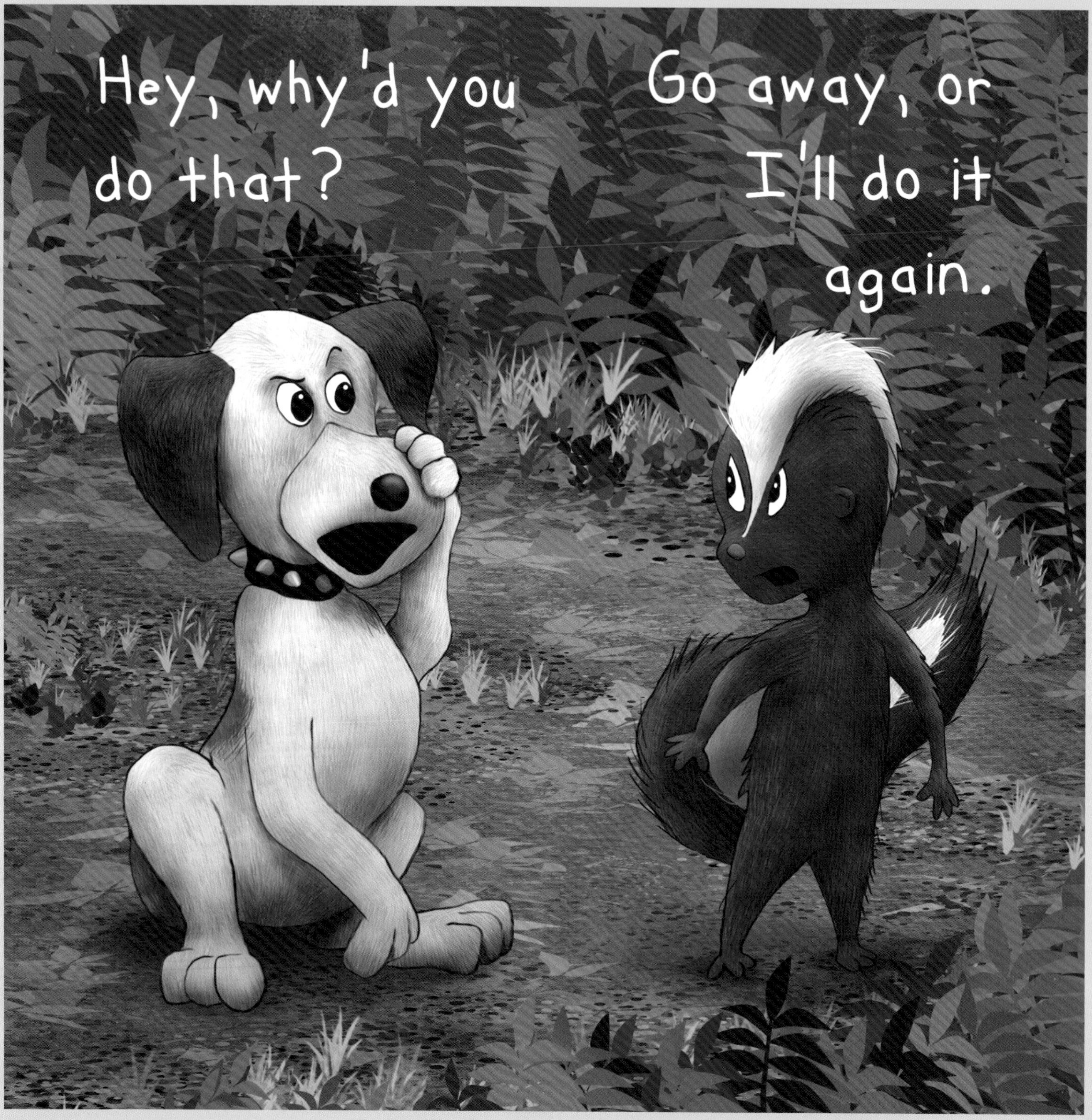
Hey, why'd you do that?
Go away, or I'll do it again.

I don't like what dog did with the barking and the growling and the running around and making noise! It's very scary, and I don't like it. I don't like when bad things happen. I don't like it at all!

rrr..rib...

I have to go to the bathroom.

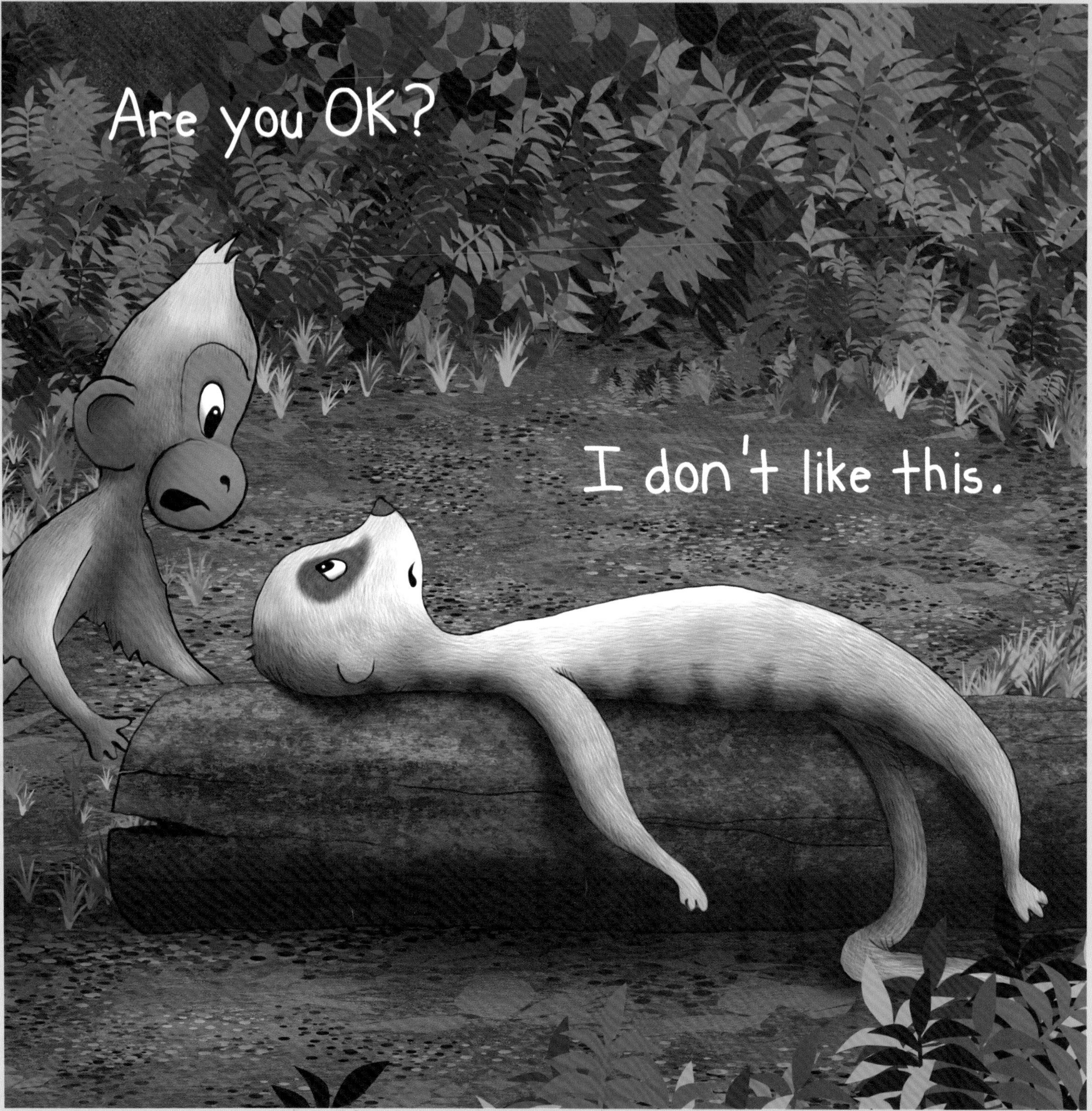
Are you OK?
I don't like this.

Oh, it seems
like you all got upset,
but you show how you
feel in different ways.

Let's think together
about what might help.

I know I look prickly. People sometimes worry that I might poke them, but I won't. I might get frustrated or a little mad because it's hard when things get crazy, but I won't hurt you.

Yes, that's true.
You don't like it
when things are loud.

When dog barked,
I don't think he
meant to scare you.
He was just trying to
show what he would do
if anyone tried to
bother him.

That's ok. You are learning, and we will help you learn. We want this to be a safe place where you don't need to bark or growl.

Or bite.

That's true. Biting is not safe. Sometimes it is hard for us to talk about what is going on inside us or figure out how we can calm down.

When you feel scared, or when you have other hard feelings like

Sad

Scared

Angry

sad, angry, frustrated, embarrassed, or ashamed, what do you do?

Embarrassed

Frustrated

Ashamed

I hide...

...and my tummy hurts.

I remember what my Mommy says. She says we should share our feelings and talk about what scares us.

Oh, and sometimes I eat. Nuts make me feel better...

Oh, and I don't sleep very well.

...and sometimes I talk too much.

I lose my voice, and all I can say is croak croak. I want to say more. I want to yell and say how scared I am, but all that comes out is croak.

I jump up and run fast...

...and sometimes I get hurt.

I become a
real stinker.

I find someone to
hold onto and hug.
Some people don't
like it when I
do that.

I pretend I'm not here,
but pretty soon I'm not
pretending. I really feel
like I'm not here, and
I don't know where I am.

You have all been through a lot, and it makes sense that you feel this way, but it also seems like you need help, so you don't keep feeling this way.

Maybe we can learn new things to do that help us when we feel scared or mad or sad.

That year, all the little animals learned lots of things. They learned how to write their names. They learned how to play fun games.

And very, very importantly, they learned what they could do when they were scared, angry, sad and feeling bad inside.

Music helps me calm down.

I still like
to run, but
I also found a
safe place where I
can be calm and snuggle.

I talked to my mom,
and she said she was
very sorry that
someone hurt me.

This makes me
feel much
better.

I will keep you safe
and make sure no
one ever hurts
you again.

I play water ball with friends and that
makes me feel so good.

My dad said that bad things don't usually happen and that makes me feel better.

ahhh...whhhh...

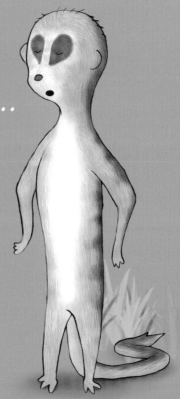

I learned to breathe. When I get scared, I pay attention to the air going in and out of my body and that helps me calm down.

I learned I'm really a cool skunk
and not a little stinker, and
I have friends who care
about me and want
me around.

I learned
that even though
people sometimes
go away, there
are people I love
who always
come back.

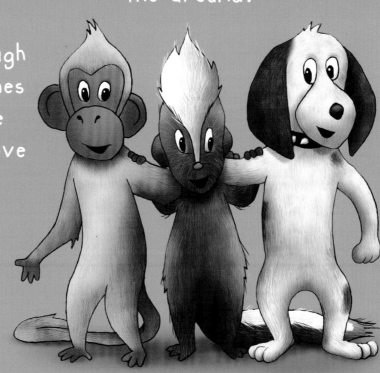

I learned I
can trust
some people.

I find that a cup of tea and a little support helps me.

And I learned that it's good to talk about things...

...sometimes.

Chandra combines her love of story and cute creatures with her training in clinical psychology. She has co-authored over 20 publications related to trauma and diversity-informed practice and has over 10 years of experience conducting trainings nationally and internationally. She also has a lifetime mission to bake 1000 pies, and a pie in all 50 states.

As a boy, Erich was always interested in cartoons and character design. In his professional career, he has created visual effects for movies like Rango, Harry Potter, The Avengers, Star Wars and many others. He is also a singer, songwriter, music producer and founding member of the local San Francisco band, District 8.

For more information about the impact of stressful
and traumatic events on children and how grown-ups can help
please visit nctsn.org

For more information about the stories and additional resources
please visit piploproductions.com